# Chinese New Year

## Dianne M. MacMillan

**Reading Consultant:**

Michael P. French, Ph.D.
Bowling Green State University

*—Best Holiday Books—*

ENSLOW PUBLISHERS, INC.

| | |
|---|---|
| Bloy St. & Ramsey Ave. | P.O. Box 38 |
| Box 777 | Aldershot |
| Hillside, N.J. 07205 | Hants GU12 6BP |
| U.S.A. | U.K. |

## Acknowledgments

*The author wishes to thank Ms. Verna Tang, reference librarian at the Chinese Information and Cultural Center, New York, for her careful review of the manuscript; and Ms. Yihua Wang, lecturer in Chinese, University of California, Los Angeles, for her review of the Chinese language and pronunciations used in the text.*

**Library of Congress Cataloging-in-Publication Data**

MacMillan, Dianne.
    Chinese New Year / Dianne M. MacMillan.
       p. cm. — (Best holiday books)
    Includes index.
    ISBN 0-89490-500-7
    1. Chinese New Year—Juvenile literature. 2. Chinese New Year—United States—Juvenile literature. 3. Chinese Americans—Social life and customs—Juvenile literature.
    [1. Chinese New Year. 2. Chinese New Year—United States. 3. Chinese Americans—Social life and customs.] I. Title. II. Series.
GT4905.M33  1994                   93-46183
394.2'61—dc20                    CIP
                                  AC

Printed in the United States of America

10 9 8 7 6 5 4 3 2 1

**Illustration Credits:** Bonnie Rhodes, p. 8; Dianne M. MacMillan, pp. 6, 11, 12, 15, 17, 21, 22, 24, 26, 28, 29, 30, 32, 34, 35, 40; © 1993 Donald Jones Photography, pp. 4, 36; Sheryl Schindler/Donald Jones Photography, p. 38.

**Cover Illustration:** Charlott Nathan

# Contents

The golden dragon is coming. Happy New Year! Gong xi fa cai!

# "Gong Xi Fa Cai"

Bang! Pop! Bang! The sound of fireworks is everywhere. A huge dragon made from paper and silk winds its way down the street. In many cities across the United States, people gather to watch the dragon parade. Children laugh as the dragon weaves back and forth. It moves to the beat of big drums. The large drums ride on platforms with wheels. Men hold the dragon up high with their arms or sticks. Bang! Pop! Bang! The dragon shakes its head and almost appears to be alive.

It is the Chinese New Year. Everyone along the parade route shouts, "Gong xi fa cai" (Kung hsi fa tsai). This means "Best wishes and congratulations!" It also means "Have a good year!" or "Happy New Year!" For Chinese people all around the world, this is an important holiday.

For thousands of years the Chinese have celebrated the new year as a spring festival. It is a time for families and friends to visit. Homes and stores are swept clean. Red banners hang from doorways. There are special foods. Children receive gifts of money in small red

This entrance is in front of a Chinese shopping area. Many Chinese Americans live in Chinatowns in large cities.

envelopes. The color red is everywhere. It stands for joy and happiness.

In Chinatowns in large cities, the dragon parade ends many days of celebrating. The parade is a blend of old and new ideas. There are marching bands and beauty queens. But last of all comes the dragon with the firecrackers. Chinese believe the noise from the exploding firecrackers will scare away the evil spirits. Then they will surely have a happy new year.

The Chinese use twelve different animals to stand for each year. Find the year that you were born. Some people believe that a person born in the year of a certain animal will act in some ways like that animal.

## *How the Holiday Began*

The Chinese have celebrated the New Year for thousands of years. The People's Republic of China is a huge country found on the continent of Asia. Long ago most of the people in China were farmers. Everyday life followed the cycles of planting and harvest. The New Year's festival was held after the fall harvest and before the start of the spring planting season.

Today Chinese people also live in other countries like Taiwan and Hong Kong. Many live in the United-States and Canada. But everyone likes to celebrate Chinese New Year.

The Chinese use a calendar based on the moon. A new moon is the beginning of a month. A full moon is the middle of a month. Chinese

New Year is the first day of the first month of the Chinese calendar. Each year the holiday falls sometime between January 21 and February 19.

The Chinese use twelve different animals to stand for each year. After twelve years, the cycle of animals begins again. The animals are the rat, ox, tiger, rabbit, dragon, snake, horse, sheep or ram, monkey, rooster, dog, and pig. The year 1994 is the year of the dog. The year of the pig is 1995. Pictures of the animal of the new year are part of the decorations. If it was the year of the tiger, pictures of tigers would be on banners. Children would carry red balloons with tigers on them. Some people believe that a person born in the year of a certain animal will act in some ways like that animal. For example, a person born in the year of the dog is thought to be loyal and dependable and also good at keeping a secret.

The year 1993 was the year of the rooster. The United States Postal Service printed a special stamp for the Chinese New Year. The stamp has a yellow rooster on a red background. On the left side in Chinese writing, it says, "Year of the Rooster." The right edge of the stamp has the words "Happy New Year." This was the first and only New Year's stamp that the U.S. Post Office has ever printed.

The most recent year of the dog is 1994. A person born in the year of the dog is thought to be loyal and dependable.

This wooden statue is in a Chinese store. Chinese shopkeepers sweep and clean their stores before the New Year begins.

## *Getting Ready for the New Year*

Some Chinese-American families celebrate on just New Year's Day. Other families follow old ways and traditions. (Tradition means to do the same thing in the same way year after year.) These families will prepare for the holiday weeks before it begins. Then they might celebrate for many days after New Year's Day, ending with the final celebration—the Golden Dragon Parade. Whichever way the family chooses to celebrate, it is always a time for fun and a new beginning.

A week before the New Year, shopkeepers or business owners sweep and clean their place of business. Families clean their homes. Everyone joins in the housecleaning. This is a way of sweeping out the old and welcoming in the new. Children help by sweeping, dusting, and carrying out trash. Once the New Year begins, it is thought to be bad luck to clean until the celebration is over. People believe that good luck arrives with the New Year. If they were to clean, they might sweep out or scrub away some of the good luck.

Many Chinese people believe in good or bad luck. During the New Year, they want to do only those things that they believe will bring good luck. Some people put away all of their scissors and knives. They do not want to risk "cutting their luck" in the New Year.

Once the house is clean, it is time to decorate. New Year's pictures called Nian hua (Ni-en hua) are hung. People hang red banners that say "good luck" in Chinese writing. On the walls are paper scrolls that have poems written on them. These poems are always hung in pairs. They are written in

Chinese characters and have good wishes for the family in the coming year.

Fruit and flowers fill the homes. Fruit is an important symbol of the New Year. (A symbol stands for an idea.) The family puts a plate of oranges in the center of the table. The oranges are stacked in a pyramid shape. Oranges are a symbol of good fortune. Red apples are a symbol of good luck because of their red color.

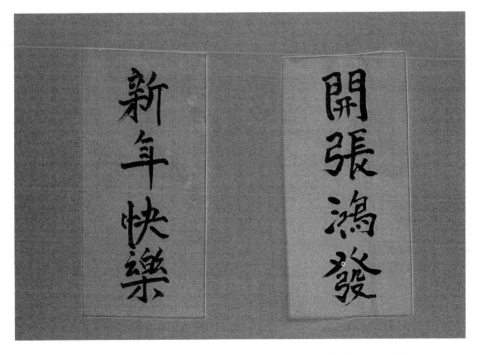

People hang red banners that say good luck in Chinese writing.

Families put spring flowers into vases. They use any flower that blooms at this time of year. Favorites are the plum blossom and the water narcissus. The plum blossom is a symbol of long life and courage. Many believe that if the water narcissus blooms on New Year's Day, then good fortune will belong to the family for the next twelve months.

Now that the house is ready, it is time to say good-bye to the kitchen god, Zao wang (Tsao wang). Many Chinese believe that the kitchen god is a spirit that lives in their homes. The job of the kitchen god is to give a report to the heavens about how the family has behaved for the past year.

Long ago in China people believed that the kitchen god left the house on the twenty-third day of the last month of the year. On this night, the family would give the kitchen god a dinner with sweet foods and honey. Some families have an altar with a statue or picture of the kitchen god. The altar may be a small table or shelf. The family places sugar cane, oranges, and honey on the altar so the kitchen god will say only sweet things about them. They offer a prayer and then burn the picture of the kitchen god and set off firecrackers. The kitchen god leaves on his journey with the noise from the firecrackers. Some people believe the kitchen god will return the first day of the new year.

Families put oranges stacked in a pyramid on their tables. Oranges are a symbol of good fortune.

The kitchen god has left. The homes and shops are clean and ready. Now it is time for the people to get themselves ready for the New Year. Families shop for new clothes. Boys may get haircuts. Getting a haircut at this time of year will bring good luck for the next twelve months. The color red is everywhere. Special foods are cooked or bought. A New Year's cake called Nian gao (Ni-en kao) is a favorite. Chinese shopkeepers decorate their stores with poems written on red paper scrolls. People pay any bills that they owe. Shopkeepers collect all their money. Everyone wants to get everything finished before the year ends.

# New Year's Eve

Finally it is New Year's Eve. The children are excited. This is the most important time for families. Grandparents, aunts, uncles, cousins, parents, and children all call it a reunion or "join-together" dinner. This is the one time during the year that everyone can see all the family members together. If someone is unable to join the family, a place is set for them along with an empty chair. This is a symbol that the person is with them. Families also remember and honor their ancestors before sitting down to dinner. (Ancestors are family members who are no longer living.)

Some families are too large to fit in one home. They may gather together in a restaurant.

Everything smells delicious. The families will eat fish, poultry, pork, beef, vegetables, and noodles. Even though the food tastes wonderful, some of it will be left on purpose. The food that is left is thought to be lucky. It will be saved and eaten by the family on New Year's Day.

Sometimes people seal the doors and windows of their homes with red paper on New Year's Eve. They believe this will seal in the good luck. Children are allowed to stay up as late as they can on New Year's Eve. This is a special treat. An old Chinese saying says that the longer the children stay up, the longer their parents will live.

At midnight the kitchen god is welcomed back home with fireworks. Food is offered to the gods. Younger members in the family will bow and pay their respect to their parents and older relatives. They are given gifts of good luck money in small red envelopes called Ya sui quian (Ya sui chi-en). The envelopes have dollars and larger bills in them. Throughout the holiday, the children and all unmarried adults will receive Ya sui quian from their married relatives.

Children and unmarried adults receive good luck money in small red envelopes during Chinese New Year.

These professional dancers are from Taiwan. There are lots of performances to watch during Chinese New Year.

## New Year's Day

In the morning, the good luck seals on doors and windows are broken. Everyone is very careful about what they say or do on New Year's Day. They try to be as good as they can. No one uses bad words or manners. Everyone tries to think good thoughts and speak kind words. It is believed that what happens on this day will decide what the family's luck will be for the rest of the year.

New clothes are put on, and the visiting begins. Everywhere you can hear people saying, "Gong xi fa cai!" Families visit grandparents first, then friends. The guests bring New Year's gifts. A gift may be a potted flowering plant or a special treat like melon seeds, candied fruit, or a New Year's cake.

Families have special foods to welcome their visitors. A tray of sweets is offered. There are eight different foods on the tray. Each food has a special meaning. Some of the foods are candied lotus seed, candied melon, candied coconut, and watermelon seeds. The lotus seed

Chinese New Year is a time for family and friends. Many families attend special shows on this holiday.

comes from a large flower that grows in water. The seeds stand for children. The melon seeds stand for good growth and health. The candied coconut stands for togetherness.

The entire day is spent enjoying family and friends. It is a fun and joyful way to begin the New Year.

This woman performs a traditional Chinese folk dance. It is part of the Chinese New Year celebration.

## *More Celebrations*

For the next week the visiting continues. There are more dinners with family and friends. In China people have a three-day holiday. They will spend their time going to the movies or the opera. Chinese opera is as loved by the Chinese people as baseball or football is by Americans. They may also watch kung fu or other martial arts. In the United States, Chinese Americans may have to work during the New Year's holiday. But they still find ways to celebrate.

Many American cities have a Chinatown. This is where many Chinese Americans live. The buildings, stores, and signs make the area look like it is part of the country of China. During the New Year holiday, everyone likes to go to Chinatown. Girls dance traditional Chinese dances. They are dressed in beautiful silk dresses. People watch Chinese boxing. There are art exhibits, kung fu contests, and lion dancers.

The lion dancers carry a large, funny head of a lion. It is made from paper and glue. The

Many large cities have a Chinatown. This mall is filled with Chinese shops and restaurants.

Everyone loves to watch the lion dance during Chinese New Year. The dancers move to the beat of a big drum.

dancers move to the beat of a giant drum. There are also gongs and symbols. People take turns making the paper lion's head swerve and bob. Chinese poets wrote about the lion dance over one thousand years ago. Dancers will dance in front of businesses and homes. With the loud drums beating, the lion dancers scare away evil

There are many performances to watch during Chinese New Year.

spirits and bring good luck to the shopkeepers. When the lion opens its mouth, people put money inside. They believe that by giving money to the lion they will be blessed with joy and good fortune.

Most celebrations last for seven days. During the New Year celebration, everyone adds one year to his or her age regardless of when their birthday is. Long ago in China birthdays were not as important as the New Year.

Some American schools celebrate Chinese New Year with special activities and projects. These children have made lion masks from paper plates.

## *School Celebrations*

Some American schools have special activities during Chinese New Year. Children talk about how the Chinese celebrate the holiday. They learn about Chinese traditions in both China and the United States. With paper plates and colorful paper, boys and girls make lion masks.

Many children learn how to write "Happy New Year" using Chinese writing. Chinese writing does not have letters. It uses strokes that form small pictures called characters. A character stands for an idea or a thing. There are 50,000 different characters in Chinese writing.

Sometimes Chinese dancers come to the school and perform. They have beautiful

This boy and girl are learning to write "Happy New Year" using Chinese writing.

costumes and are very graceful. Then everyone gets to eat Chinese food. There may be rice, noodles, and egg rolls. Everyone enjoys celebrating the Chinese New Year.

Chinese writing uses strokes that form small pictures called characters.

In many cities across the United States people gather to watch the dragon parade on Chinese New Year.

## The Golden Dragon Parade in Chinatown

After a week of visiting friends and family, eating good food, and going to many Chinese events, Chinese New Year is almost over. But the holiday goes out with a big bang: the Golden Dragon Parade! Thousands of firecrackers are set off. They light up the night sky with colorful designs. At times there is so much smoke you cannot see the dragon. Some children and even adults hold their ears because of all the noise. Having fireworks on holidays is an old Chinese tradition. Lots of people use fireworks during holiday celebrations. But the Chinese people invented gunpowder and fireworks.

Hours before the parade starts, people gather

Thousands of firecrackers are set off during the parade.

along the sidewalks. Everyone wants to get a good spot to watch. Families and friends are talking and laughing. Finally the parade begins. Marching bands play music as they pass by. Some marchers carry banners with pictures of the animal for this New Year. Singers sing traditional songs. Acrobats perform for the crowd. Famous and important Chinese Americans ride in open cars and wave to the crowds. People in the crowds cheer and wave back to them. As each group marches by, the excitement grows. Everyone is waiting for the dragon. The arrival of the dragon is the best part of the parade.

The Chinese believe the dragon is a sacred or holy animal. It was the sign of the Chinese emperors (or rulers) of long ago. The dragon is a symbol of strength and goodness. It appears once each year in the parade. The dragon's appearance is a way of wishing everyone peace, good fortune, and good luck for the coming year.

The dragon is a symbol of strength and goodness. It appears in the parade, but people think about the dragon all through the New Year's celebration.

Fireworks continue to explode. The noise grows louder and louder. Everyone cheers and claps. The dragon is coming. Bang! Pop! Bang! Happy New Year! Gong xi fa cai!

## *Note to Parents, Teachers, and Librarians*

---

The Chinese words used in this book are in the Mandarin dialect. Mandarin is the major dialect spoken in China and the one used in all publications outside of China.

# Glossary

**altar**—A small table or shelf used in religious ceremonies.

**ancestors**—Family members who are no longer alive.

**characters**—Small pictures made from brush strokes that make up Chinese writing.

**Gong xi fa cai**—"Happy New Year" in the Chinese language.

**lotus seed**—The seed that comes from a large flower that grows in water.

**Nian gao**—Special New Year's cake.

**Nian hua**—New Year's pictures.

**reunion**—The act of joining together again. The dinner on New Year's Eve is called a reunion dinner.

**tradition**—Something that is done in the same way year after year.

**Ya sui qian**—Small red envelopes that have good luck money in them.

**Zao wang**—The Chinese kitchen god.

# Index